# The Voice of Washington Elementary

## An Anthology of Poems

1st WORLD
LIBRARY
Literary Society

# The Voice of Washington Elementary
## An Anthology of Poems

© 1st World Library – Literary Society, 2004
1100 North 4th St. Suite 131, Fairfield, Iowa 52556
Tel: 641-209-5000 • Fax: 641-209-3001 • Web: www.1stworldlibrary.org

First Edition

LCCN: 2004099106

ISBN: 1-59540-900-9

Readers can contact www.1stworldlibrary.org for information on services provided by 1stWorld Library-Literary Society:

Readers interested in supporting literacy through
sponsorship, donations or
membership please contact:
literacy@1stworldlibrary.org
Check us out at: www.classiclibrary.ORG
and start downloading free ebooks today.

THE VOICE OF
WASHINGTON ELEMENTARY - 2004
IS SPONSORED BY:


CENTRAL VALLEY BANK

LIBERTYVILLE SAVINGS BANK

WAL-MART STORES

SUPPORTING HIGHER LITERACY IN IOWA

# DEDICATION BY MAYOR ED MALLOY

I suppose every mayor believes that his or her city is made up of the brightest and most creative citizens. That the community is special because what it produces is of a higher quality than any other town. Every mayor supports and embraces the good works that come from every corner of the city and takes great pride in boasting about its accomplishments.

The beauty of a truly creative community is that those accomplishments come in a myriad of forms, large and small, visible and invisible, recognized and unrecognized. Community projects are sponsored and performed by service clubs, schools, churches, special committees and individuals. It is quite special when the youngest of our citizens contribute the most delightful of achievements.

The anthology of poems from the Washington Elementary School is an inspiration to behold. Publishing an entire book of poems would be a major accomplishment for any collection of people, let alone first through fifth graders. The poems of each grade reflect the growth and appreciation of life around them and their budding skills of expression. From the analogies of love and fire in Shannon Barker's *Fire,* to the whimsical acrobatic tale in Monica Schubick's *Twirling,* the poetry is magical and heartwarming.

If this is the Voice of Washington Elementary then our city is most fortunate to get a preview of the talent and creativity that will grow and sustain our community for many years to come. I trust that the adults who wrote these verses in their youth will look back and be proud of what they accomplished back then, and will appreciate how it shaped them into who they are now.

ED MALLOY
MAYOR, FAIRFIELD, IOWA

# FOREWORD

"Writing is the most personal of the "3 R's" and poetry is the most personal form of writing. Students, parents, teachers, and friends will enjoy this collection now ------ and even more in the future as a record of the thoughts and emotions of Washington Elementary students."

JIM RUBIS
DIRECTOR, FAIRFIELD PUBLIC LIBRARY

# INTRODUCTION

"The voices of our children speak to us in many ways. This collection of poetry was created by the students of Washington school for their enjoyment, as a learning experience and for your pleasure. Many of our students and staff were reluctant to become involved in this project. However, as the process evolved, both the students and staff became more and more enthusiastic about what was happening in the classrooms. Students started cranking out a variety of material that showed both insight and a creative thinking side that many had not displayed in the past. Staff became more excited to see the enjoyment the students had in producing, as well as sharing their writing.

This has been an outstanding project for our whole school community and we recommend it to others as a positive teaching aid for writing and self discovery. One teacher said," I didn't think my class (students) would be able to participate in this project, but they proved me wrong. This has been a great experience for us. My students really surprised me! I will incorporate this poetry unit in my class next year."

We hope you will enjoy reading and pondering the thoughts of our children."

PRINCIPAL DUSANEK
WASHINGTON ELEMENTARY SCHOOL

# PREFACE

"For we children, the most beautiful thoughts are already poetic. We are magical, fresh, exciting and wise enough to know that we can change the whole world by just being ourselves. Our feelings are special. We are tender and we carry our own colors, each different with different shades. The poems that follow are written by children and selected by children as winners of an ongoing poetry competition. These poems are intended to introduce the wonders of poetry to the new generation."

ANYA AND AMAN CHARLES.
CHILDREN'S POETRY EDITORS,
1ST WORLD LIBRARY.

*Poetry ....is the art of words.*

# FIRE

The blazing fire
Blazing so bright
Will someday expire
In the world

The blazing fire
In my heart
Will never expire

In my heart there is love

Some people say love is a myth
But love is fire burning inside
For love is a beautiful gift
That not everyone can receive

Love is fire
And fire is love


Shannon Baker

# THE ALPHABET ZOO

When we went to the alphabet zoo,
I saw a walking W.

After that I saw a tree,
With a swinging Z and a bussing B.

I walked down a path so far,
That at the end I saw a growling R.

On the left of the way,
I saw a swimming K and jumping J

They were funny and I wasn't blue,
Until I saw a slimy Q.

I had a blast, the day was fun,
Now it was time for me to run.

I was sad until I knew,
That I had seen a friend named U.

I told U all about how it had begun,
Now it was time for U to have fun.

So enjoy, my friend, it was great,
Meeting the Alphabet animals at the alphabet
gate.

## Mason Ellis

# TWIRLING

Once there was a girl
Who loved to twirl
She twirled at school
She twirled by the mule
She twirled on the stairs
Even twirled on chairs

One day she said
I see spots in my head
So she went to the doctor
Whose name was Smoctor
He looked in her ear
Brains upside down,my dear

She never twirls now
She can't remember how


## Monica Schubick

# DESERTED

We are lost, we are lonely,
We don't know what to do
It's just going to be me and you

Where will we go
What will we do
I'm confused and so afraid

Why did they leave us?
Why  today?


Lani Eversage

# LIBERTY

Statute of Liberty
Standing for freedom
Symbol of America
Brought to us from France

## Vincent Horras

# MAY I GO TO THE BATHROOM?

I need to go to the bathroom.
The clock is ticking fast.
Come on, pick me,
Or I will never last.

Come on, say my name
Say my name
I need to go really, really bad
And…

Uh oh……

Brooke Stever

# MY FAMILY

My family will always support me
Like when I'm safe in a house
They always will help me
Always will love me
Will always be so helpful
If I did not have a family
I would not accomplish anything
So you should remember
Your family is the most important thing
That should be in your life.

Michael Gookin

# ABC ANIMALS

Antelopes acting angry at alligators
Bucks bouncing bats before breakfast
Canaries carrying colors, creating chaos
Dogs dunking delicious donuts
Electric elephants eating eggs
Freaky frogs floating forever
Giraffes gawking at gymnasts
Horses have hair houses
Iguanas in icky igloos
Jaguars jumping in January
Kangaroos kicking kings
Lions line up little leopards
Monkeys make messes out of the mail
Newts, not nice
Octopus on olives outside
Peacocks phone people
Quails quite quiet
Rabbits really ride in rallies
Snakes slither and saunter slowly south
Toads thank truckers
Unicorns use umbrellas
Vipers violin very valiantly
Weasels writing who, what, when, where

X-ray fish exit extingly
Yaks yakking, yawning and yelling
Zebras zig-zagging

Jordan Whitney

# THE POLLUTION OF NATURE

The trees blow with fright
With the sadness of nature
And howling of the winds

A haiku by **Spencer Wiseman**

# A CUP OF TEA

Some things are fun
For example: to run,
Some things are not,
Like untying a knot

So you must see,
That a cup of tea
Isn't bad.
When you are sad
Bring a cup of tea
For you and me

Anonymous

# THAT KID

There's a kid that no one
Pays any attention to
Kids make up rumors
That kid hears them.

That kid hides in shadows
So no one will see him
Some kids wonder if that kid
Has any parents

That kid did, but they died
In a car accident
He's just waiting for his turn to go
Just like his parents did
A long time ago.

And everybody still calls him that kid.


Jessica Wood

# MEXICO

Hard working people
Really hot days
Spicy tacos and soccer players
Visiting family

Matthew Juraez

# STARS

Stars are in the sky
Dancing all the time

They are a light to you
and to me
Right?

Do you disagree?
They are protectors

## Kassie Myers

# DENNIS RODMAN'S HAIR

Its here its there its everywhere
Dennis Rodman's red, red hair

I go to the mall
What do I see?
Dennis Rodman in front of me

It's here it's there it's everywhere
Dennis Rodman's red, red hair

I go home
What do I see?
Dennis Rodman in front of me
It's here it's there it's everywhere

I go upstairs, come back down
What do I see?
I see Dennis Rodman in front of me
Watching T.V.
Asleep in the chair
Oh what a scare

Corbin Harwood

# MY FAT?

There once lived a cat
Really fat
One day they said
you need to go on a diet
He went on a riot
I don't care if I'm a fat cat

## Anonymous

# HAMSTER CANCER

There once was a man who had cancer
Who got it from his old little hamster
His hamster  died
The old man  cried
But now he has no more cancer


Ramses Alonso

# MAKING A POEM

My mom
Smelled like a baboon
When she got home
From Africa
She picked up the baboon seed


Mrs. Dicky's 1st grade

# HEAVEN

Heaven is what you want it to be.
Heaven is believing.
Don't you see?
Heaven is loving him.
Don't worry.
We all sin..
Heaven is your life
Eternally.
Heaven is faith
Christians go there,
thinking "finally."

## Danielle Hannes

# PENCILS

Pencils
Erasers help
Writing words on paper.
Makes me feel good and so happy.
Pencils


Luis Giron

# MOTHER I LOVE YOU

Even if a day goes by
With out me saying I love you
I don't want a second to pass
Without you knowing I do

When you are happy
I'll love you with a joyful heart
And when you are sad I'll love
You with a heavy heart


Michelle Spears

# THE WIND

The wind and the breeze
They glide with great ease

It flies with beautiful grace
With its cool touch upon your face

It dances with the trees and the flowers
Even with the warm spring showers

It giggles and plays
With the sun's warm rays

If it ever goes away
The wind will come back another day


Jweal Lazty

# LUNCH TIME

Our lunch here is from outer space
Endangering the human race

The deadly tuna casserole
Made me roll right out the door

The carrot cake –don't dare to try it
The apple pie almost caused a riot

Good thing there's a sub cook today
And I hope the special isn't hay

Don't listen to this deadly rhyme
But lunch is still my favorite time


Jessica Enright

# TURTLE

Turtle
Hard, smelly
Swims, slow, crawl
Big, small, cute, neat
Tortoise

Alec Stoner

# ALLISON

Allison
Looking a little shy
Loving animals
Including the
Skunk

o.k. maybe
not the skunk


## Allison Angstead

# LIKE A ROSE

my life is like a red, red rose

fresh and beautiful
the sun big and yellow
the sky blue and quiet
clouds moving slowly
stars bright as fire

my life is quiet and slow, like a red, red rose


Priscila Capetillo

# THE GIRL

The girl was very vicious
Even though she was rich as a princess

She turned around with a frown
And beat me with her crown

the girl

## Logan Hoffman

# THE COLORS OF THE RAINBOW

Red, is meant for a big juicy apple.
Orange for a basketball flying through a hoop.
Yellow, the sun shining upon us at the beach.
Green, reading under a tree on the grass.
Blue, the big beautiful sky.
And purple, the clouds at sunset.

It seems every color is meant
For something.


Haven Willliam Tichy

# THE OCEAN

The ocean at day
The ocean at noon
The ocean at night
The ocean so bright

Trevor Williams

# A POEM ABOUT NEW YORK CITY

buildings that even Bigfoot would consider huge
cars honking their horns because of a traffic jam
hot dogs from a Yankees' basketball game
  concession stand
fumes coming from factories surrounding
  me on all sides
cement from well built streets and houses
I feel in my heart
that is where I want to be.


Max Sloat

# DREAMS

P.b and j, oh yes, I say.
I eat a sandwich every day.

The peanut butter, so smooth and creamy,
The bread, so very hot and steamy.

The jelly spread as big as a dish,
Reminds me of caviar, canned eggs of a fish.

I take a bite, and yuck! It tastes sour.
Someone left it out for over an hour!

I wash my mouth, the taste is still there,
So I go outside to get some fresh air.

Then next day I wake up stiff.
I smell something awful, but then I sniff.

I smell bubble gum, cherries, even ice cream!
But then, I wake up, …in a dream.


Kahlise Rotondi

# EXPRESSIONS

Happy, sad, feeling good, or bad,
You're always feeling expressions.

Embarrassed, shocked,
or feeling like you just had you're shot
You're always feeling expressions.

Angry, depressed, or mad
because you have a sharp pain in your chest
You're always feeling expressions.

Expressions come in the day and the night.
Sometimes they will give another person
  quite a fright.
But no matter what
You are always feeling expressions.


Sunita Martin

# FAMILY

family
funny, nice
playful,  helpful , clean , messy
giving, sharing , using
softball, basketball
family


Erin Thompson

# THE ARMY

If you are gold and blue
Come on and join the crew
If our colors are orange and yellow,
We will work just like brothers.
If you are to fail,
We will tell your mom that you wailed.
If you make it,
We will shake it.


Britni Sherman

# THE EARTH

The flower smell
The seashore shell

The birds with wings
The bees that sting

We love the Earth without a doubt,
Even the parts that have a drought

Adam Gevovk

# GRANDMA

My grandma
Worked on her house
Yesterday
In Fairfield
So she can have somewhere to live


## Mrs. Dicky's 1st grade

# KEELI

She is so stinky.
She has a binkey

She plays with others
She was born in October

She loves toys
She Barks at boys

## Skyler Bartholomew

# RATCHET

Looks like a mutated fox
Feels furry
He's cool

Makes my heart pump
Hard

Smells like sweat and a fox
Tastes like fur

He makes mean jokes


Tyler Breeding

# MY CLASS

My
Class
Is
Really
Nice
Kara
And
Allison
And
Brooke
And
Emily
And
Tanner
They
Play
With
Me
At
Recess
And
They
Sit
By

Me
At
Lunch

# Aubreann Loving

# CRAZY

I'm going crazy
I'm making a valentine
It has to be perfect!
It shouldn't be too big,
And it shouldn't be too small.
I am going crazy!
I can't even breathe!!!
I think I'll get some ice cream,
So I can calm down.


Aubreann Loving

# CRICKETS

green and joyful hopping around the grass
strange and unusual smooth and bumpy
completely wonderful at night
tastes bad like spinach
smells weird and fragrant
means a lot to me


Sam Dovico

# MRS. D

Mrs. Dickey
she is funny
at school
when she visits Mrs. Kluver's room
she does funny dances and sings songs

## Dyllan Light

# BASKETBALL!

I can see the players passing the ball to each
other
Feel the bumps on the ball
Squeaking shoes on the ground
Stinky gross sweat
Feel your heart getting ready to burst out
  of your chest
In the last seconds
And then, taste the dry roof of your mouth


## Chelsea Haynes

# EVERYTHING

Everything
Sports, animals, plants,
People, books, colors, cars,
Schools, everything ,everything never ends.


Kayla Ledger

# ME

I'm happy to be me you see
It's me I want to be

I'm not mean, or green,
But I am glean and clean

I am fine and nine
I do not whine

I want to be in band
Because it is grand

So that's why I want to be me.


Haley Williams

# RHYMING FUN

Box on fox fox on box
Book on hook hook on book
Feet on beet beet on feet
Dog on hog hog on dog
Lock on rock rock on lock
Log on frog frog on log
Moss on sauce sauce on moss
Horse on coarse coarse on horse
Pup on cup cup on pup
Top on pop pop on top
Sofa on loofa loofa on sofa
Hat on bat bat on hat
Hot on pot pot on lot

Dalton Price

# DAD

my dad
works on cars
everyday
he has built cars his whole life.


## Dakota Weeks

# MOM AND ME

I think of us lying on the bay,
Watching all the seaweed sway.

Every time we go out to play,
I always hold your hand along the way.

When I am sick,
You know what to give me,
And you cure it quick!

I love you, Mom!


Michaela Burmeier

# MOM

my mom
she works really hard
at Cambridge and George's
almost everyday
we need money so we can move into a house


Robert Kloski

# ASTRONAUTS

The astronauts are blasting off!
   3,2,1,
   blast off!!
   Way ,way in the sky...........
   A rocket ship
They are in space already,
   Wow,
The moon!
A meteorite!!!!!!!

Tanner Cook

# THE FIRST FIVE MONTHS

It's January! Snow is here!
Time for the new year!!

February, Valentine's
We can give them anytime.

March! It's Spring! Time to play!
Pretty soon it will be May.

April ! It's my birthday!
When will it be May?

May! It's finally May!
All I want to do is play!


## Coren Hucke

# BEST FRIEND

Reilly
is my best friend
at home and at school
everywhere
during the day and night
l love her and she loves me


Dakota Webber

# HELPS ALL

Mrs. Miller
helps all kids
Washington Elementary
if I need an ice pack
or to call my parents
to check our temperature
and give us lunch tickets
she is the nicest secretary


Trent Taglauer

# FAMILY

Willie
he helps me read and practice spelling
at home
after school and at night
he is my brother
he is family.

Gareth West

# APPLE

Little Apple, my cat
he carries his bowl on his back

when I set the bowl on his back
he probably thinks it is funny.


Jolea Burkhart

# MATTHEW

My name is Matthew
About every day , I see birds
Twenty –five or
Thirty –two
Having fun watching birds
Every day I watch them,
While eating lunch outside.

## Matthew Carr

# THE CRUISE

one day I went on a cruise
one guy blew a fuse
other people were
walking along
and before they knew
it they.......

blew off the boat!


Matthew Carr

# GRANDMA

grandma Birdy
she takes good care of me
everyday
she loves me very much.


Austin Hagans

# I LOVE HORSES

I love horses
Do you love horses?

I love the sound of the hooves going
Clip clop clip clop!

It feels like you're flying, almost.
The wind is in your face.

And the best part is you're free.
Just you
Your horse

Allison Angstead

# MY FAMILY

my name is Jordan
my mom's name is Gail
my dad's name is Stacy
my sister's name is Brittni

we
all
love
each
other!


Jordan Sherman

# 8:00 SOMETHING

oh ,it's 8:00 something
oh, it's almost time for something
  I can't remember
  What it's almost time for.......
"hurry up", says mom.
"it's almost time for
  school!"


Rachel Biggs

# VALENTINE'S DAY

Valentine's day will soon
   Be here!

Our class celebrates it
   Every year

Passing valentine cards
   And candy too –

Fun or what? #1
   Valentine's day is cool!!


Keri Schwarz

# MY FRIENDS

My friends are cool
And nice
They like me
For who I am
We play a lot
It's so fun
I like them
And they like me!


Kara Greiner

# OCTOBER, OCTOBER

I love October!
Broomsticks in the air
Witches laughing
Ghosts are falling
From black and white moons

If you're scared
Just run away!!!


Dorian Larson

# LONELY

Nicolas
Naughty boy
In a
Cage
Outside
Lonely with
A
Sock

## Nicolas Richalae

# CHINA

People carrying baskets
And working hard
Spicy chicken makes me drool
China feels like home
China is the best!

Dorian Larson

# THINGS I LIKE

I like to
go to school
to play games
and go to P.E.,
music,
and art.
I like wrestling,
baseball,
kickball,
football,
soccer,
basketball,
math!!

Jacob Heisel

# I DON'T KNOW

I don't know what to write about.
I'm writing a poem about not knowing
  what to write
A poem about.
Hoooooooooooray!!!!!
I just wrote one.
Cool!


Nicolas Rich

# RUN

See how she runs
Runs by the sun
Glides by the trees
Feeling her knees
Runs past the ants
they crawl up her pants
Hurry, hurry as she runs
To the end of all the fun

Sami Herman

# MOUNTAIN LIONS

Mountain lions are very deadly.
Very very deadly!
They're in Iowa!
They're everywhere!
They eat living humans.
They tear flesh clear off.


Landon Gamrath

# MY FAMILY IS SPECIAL TO ME

My family is special to me
Even if my sister trashes her room
She says my voice is the voice of doom

My brother is very annoying,
(very, very annoying)
My younger brother Brody isn't too bad,
Except he wakes me up in the middle of the
night

My mom tells me to clean my room
My dad tells me to help him on the farm.
I think I'm going to EXPLOde!!

Anyway,
My family is special to me!


## Allison Angstead

# HURRY! HURRY!

Oh, no!
Thanksgiving is coming and we are not ready!
Hurry! Hurry! Get the turkey!
Hurry! Hurry! Get the pie!
But how will we get the turkey?
Will we hunt it?
Will we buy it?
What will we do?
Hurry! Hurry!
Call out the Indians and the Pilgrims.
It is November.
It is Thanksgiving and we are not ready.
Hurry! Hurry! Hurry!

Aubreann Loving

# BEE, BEE, IN A TREE

Bee, Bee, In a tree.
I see you and you see me!
I love the bee in the tree,
For if I did not have it-
I would not have honey!!


Brooke Stever

# MY BAD DOG

My dog is always
Bringing my mom pinecones.

She gets in my sister's books.
She always gets in my stuff.

She drives my Mom crazy,
Though I don't care.


Landon Gamrath

# THE TWISTER

The twister was scary!
It sucked up my car!
I hoped it wouldn't get close to me,
But it wasn't far

It was colored gray,
Or reddish-brown,
It was a funnel from the sky
Touching the ground.


Coren Hucke

# DINER

Restaurant
Big, noisy
Ordering, cooking, serving,
Really good food served
Diner


Riley Hammel

# SPRING

Spring is coming
I'd like to say
It's a beautiful day
For me to play

I smell spring flowers
They smell so good
They make me think
I'm in Candyland!

## Aspen Light

# BEST

Dr. Seuss, you're the best book writer around.
Dr. Seuss, you're the best in town.
I like Cat in the Hat and Green Eggs and Ham.
Dr. seuss you're the best.


Claudia Sloat

# NIGHT

Night sky
A bright twinkling star
A big, yellow, harvest moon
In the dark,dark, sky.

### Mrs. Koch's 2<sup>nd</sup> Graders

# WINTER

Winter
Snowy, snowy,
Frost winter wonderland
Flakes falling softly


## Mrs. Koch's 2<sup>nd</sup> Graders

# WINTER IN THE INDIAN VILLAGE

I see the colorful sunset.
And I hear the wind whispering in my ear.

I feel the wind in my hair.
And I smell the smoke from the fire.

I can taste the deer that we're having for supper.


Daniel Schwarz

# PYSANKY EGGS

I see some colors
Red, blue and black
The sound of splashes
I touch the eggs.
I can smell the vinegar in the dye.
And taste candle smoke in the air.


Ashley Evard

# MOLLY

There could be no better
Dog you can see
Than my little Molly

I love her
And she loves me
We'll be together
For eternity

It turns out I was wrong
It is time for Molly
To move along


Jacquelyn Bell

# WINTER FUN

Snow is melting now,
Cardinals fly through the air,
We can have fun too!


Jonathan Anderson

# WE LOVE WASHINGTON SCHOOL

We love school !

| | |
|---|---|
| Centers | Loreena |
| Recess | Alex |
| Reading sentences | Cade |
| Sharing | Cooper |

We love school !

| | |
|---|---|
| Day 100 | Trae |
| Computers | Mackenzie |
| Lunch | Drew S |
| Teachers | Kiera |

We love school !

| | |
|---|---|
| Helping | Nathan |
| Art | Slolmon |
| Music | Sydney |
| P.E | Melissa |

We love school !

| | |
|---|---|
| Calendars | Hunter |

| | |
|---|---|
| Parties | Paige |
| Birthdays | Dylan |
| Work | Jacob |

We love school !

| | |
|---|---|
| Friends | Alexis |
| Counting by 5's | Jarrett |
| Playtime | Kyle |
| "Pledge of Allegiance" | Tistan |

We love school !

| | |
|---|---|
| Learning | Shea |
| Feeling good | Drew T |
| Happy | Macy |
| Making things | Price |

We love school !

## Mrs. Moore's Kindergarten 2004